T0086772

EXTRAVAGANT RESCUES

EXTRAVAGANT RESCUES

Poems

Brett Foster

Foreword by Jeffrey Galbraith

TRIQUARTERLY BOOKS / NORTHWESTERN UNIVERSITY PRESS

Northwestern University Press
www.nupress.northwestern.edu

Copyright 2019 by TriQuarterly Books/Northwestern University Press.
Published 2019. All rights reserved.

Printed in the United States of America

10 9 8 7 6 5 4 3 2 1

Library of Congress Cataloging-in-Publication Data

Names: Foster, Brett, 1973–2015, author. | Galbraith, Jeffrey, writer of foreword.
Title: Extravagant rescues : poems / Brett Foster ; foreword by Jeffrey Galbraith.
Description: Evanston, Ill. : TriQuarterly Books/Northwestern University Press,
    2019. | Includes bibliographical references.
Identifiers: LCCN 2019017366 | ISBN 9780810140547 (trade paper : alk. paper) |
    ISBN 9780810140554 (e-book)
Classification: LCC PS3606.O7496 A6 2019 | DDC 811.6—dc23
LC record available at https://lccn.loc.gov/2019017366

I have roared for the very disquietness of my heart.

—Psalm 38 (Miles Coverdale's translation)

Oh when the world is silent,
I hear music in the air.

. . .

—"Over My Head" (African American spiritual)

"If you see something, say something."

—Recorded TSA warning on Chicago's Metra trains

/ TOO MUCH, DEAR READER, TOO MUCH? /

CONTENTS

FOREWORD

Jeffrey Galbraith

When Brett Foster died of cancer on November 9, 2015, his work on *Extravagant Rescues* was largely complete. He had submitted the manuscript, and reached a decision on the title, well before his diagnosis in May of 2014. Earlier, in the process of assembling the manuscript, he solicited and received input from a number of friends and associates, including fellow poets and academics such as Alan Jacobs, David Wright, and Kimberly Johnson. Should he have seen the manuscript through to publication, the acknowledgments page would have been lengthy and warmly gracious. Brett nurtured community and thrived in conversation. It was his joy to correspond with others, whether in person or via notes and emails that managed to convey, in short space, the vigor and wit of his presence.

Early readers of the manuscript, myself included, felt an excitement in the new work. *Extravagant Rescues* launches us beyond the already wide bounds of *The Garbage Eater*, Brett's first book. In these poems, keen observations of the surprising or oddly humorous mix with lyrical meditations that bring classical tradition to bear on suburban middle age, powered by loosely rhyming couplets that give the work broad discursive freedom. In a letter to a friend, Brett described the collection as having "a little more swagger," with "a little jazzy mischief here and there." The first book combined Brett's Missouri upbringing with the distances he traversed as a student of early modern literature. Emblems of that combination appeared throughout *The Garbage Eater*, in Eurydice's appearance in an Ozarks cave, for instance, and in the heroic echoes of kids throwing fireworks at trains. As a longtime fan of Brett's work, I remember being surprised by the rich coherence of the book. The poems about the liturgical calendar and Christian belief became something new when framed by the startling title poem. If Brett's work tended to observe a strict decorum regarding the passions of religious belief, the portrayal of a Christian cult member challenged that propriety. Although the extremist differed from the poet, the title poem admitted to their likeness. Placed at the beginning of the collection, the poem establishes a strong orienting sympathy. Both poet and extremist can be said to have "learned to meditate on the soul's / needs," "fear[ing] / only unworthiness more than death."

The extremist's diet of judgment opens a path to the exuberance and warmth so clearly on display in this new work. *Extravagant Rescues* is astonishingly receptive, transforming its wide-ranging references into a kind of wisdom literature for the technological age, each poem providing a new concoction of parts. The poet's intelligence seizes with energetic wit on YouTube videos, oil derricks in a cornfield, the sight of bucket trucks lined up in a parking lot, even (*gasp!*) George Clooney. All become emblems giving airy edifice to hope and human limits. "We Strivers All" focuses on Nim Chimpsky, the primate test subject who was taught sign language by researchers at Columbia University in the 1970s. When we are introduced to Nim, he is on the downward slope of Fortune's wheel, wordless at middle age, wallowing at the bottom of the U-curve. The primate offers a remarkable conceit for what becomes a meditation on *vanitas*. Brett animates the trope of the washed-up pop icon, expanding beyond the simian to claim that "every man is a vanity." The poem's ending achieves a cutting beauty in this regard, leading readers away from the solaces of whimsy. In the last lines, the claim that "each self-anointed striver moves, self-deceiving" elevates with a comparison drawn from Coverdale's Psalms: "*like as it were a moth / fretting a garment.*" It is a deft stroke, which pleases as it wounds. If the wisdom of *Exuberant Rescues* is more concerned with lyricism than with the boundary lines of doctrine, it is no less convicting for that.

On the strength of *Extravagant Rescues*, it is tempting to speculate how Brett's poetry would have continued to grow had he not become ill. At the time of his death, as the new work shows, Brett had developed the ability to convey a seemingly effortless assemblage of references in the space of a single poem. What might he have accomplished? Classical learning, in the form of Renaissance humanism, would doubtless have continued to serve as a handbook of invention. A clue to Brett's method appears in an epigraph from *The Garbage Eater*. The words are those of the Italian humanist Leon Battisti Alberti, describing his concept of the universal man: "He took extraordinary and peculiar pleasure in looking at things in which there was any mark of beauty or adornment." The discipline of looking is evident in Brett's capacious powers of attention, evident in the way the poems slide easily back and forth through time and across different cultural registers. Consider how *The Garbage Eater*, for instance, draws Milton and Plotinus into the same orbit as the singer memorialized in "Trashy Elegy for the Queen of Shock Rock." For Brett, the discipline of observation gave license to what at times seemed like a mania for collecting. Brett was an avid collector not only of secondhand books but also of news accounts and human-interest stories. It was his regular practice to scour newspapers and magazines for clippings to add to his files. Sorting through folders after his death, I stifled a laugh when I came upon a group of obituaries he had collected. Cut from the *New York Times*, the folder included such gems as "Robert Degen, Had Hand in Hokey Pokey" and "Flo Gibson, Grand Dame of Audiobooks." What magic, what amalgam, did Brett plan to make with such figures? My favorite was the obituary for "Teenie Hodges, Soul Guitarist and Songwriter." I can easily imagine Mr. Hodges, a guitarist who composed with Al Green, taking the stage in one of Brett's unwritten future poems. Perhaps Brett would have him playing dulcimer strains as the dove descended on Christ at the Jordan. Or maybe he'd have him strum a chord the instant water became wine at Cana.

To place *Extravagant Rescues* alongside *The Garbage Eater* is to see how Brett continued to set larger goals for his poetry. Those close to him recognized that this ambition was the result of his searching intelligence but also a certain restlessness. While writing the poems of *Extravagant Rescues*, he was the parent of children speeding toward adolescence, a tenured professor with a mortgage. He knew the "donkey work" (his phrase) of daily toil. Perhaps for this reason *Extravagant Rescues* signals a shift in tone. There is more than a hint of darkness in the singing, as these poems seek renewal in the form of "the eyes shouting / or undergoing something tantamount // to new life for senses wasted away." Maybe it's that the imagination has become wary of its charms. In "Upon News of the Important Fossil," the creative faculty is likened to an early human tool, resembling the sharp edge of flint or, what came later, "method's first intimation." What is wrought by using the tool of imagination? How does the tool work upon those who wield it? The answer we get is deliberately vague:

> It says something, to imagine all
> remaining ahead, dizzy festival
> of ozones, phonemes, green zones, iPhones,
> charred craters of conscience, newer loneliness.

Such wariness does not lessen the moments of joy or abate the sense of play. The wonderful delirium of "Happiness, Carolina Highway," here quoted in full, demonstrates the fresh confidence that is characteristic of the collection:

I tried to sing falsetto
amid the pine and palmetto.
I had a golden god's bravado,
made bold by my Eldorado.

This song, about trying to sing, packs an outsized performance into a brief lyric. The "bravado" of the poem lies in the freedom and ease of its style, in the poised assurance that such efforts are, indeed, enough.

The day Brett died, a group of actors comprised of theater faculty and former students performed a selection of his poetry to a sold-out audience at Wheaton College's Arena Theater. The performance drew from published and unpublished poems, weaving together a narrative of Brett's stories that honored his work, the gift of his friendship, and the impact he had made on the college and the larger community. Although he attended a few rehearsals that fall, providing the actors with valuable notes and insights, Brett would not make it to opening night. As we came to realize, however, the performance was less for him than it was for those in attendance. The event of Brett's death reversed the action of giving. What was designed as a gift to the poet was suddenly transformed into a gift to all those who loved him, giving communal space to our grief. That night Brett was not there, and yet he was. Perhaps that is the most accurate description of his poems.

EXTRAVAGANT RESCUES

CONTRA BELLY

—after Persius

I never raced my verse from the jalopy lot
nor sought a double major at Parnassus U
to spring forth *ergo* an immediate poet.
Debutantes of Helicon and Perene's whitewash
I relinquish to him whose jacket photo's crowned
with fawning ivy. Of the semiliterati,
I offer up my tunes to our sponsored open mike.
Who's helping out the parrot to chirp-chirp his cheer?
Who enrolled the magpie to imitate our words?
Writer-in-residence, arbiter of "hard-won truth,"
Belly skillfully follows the spring's next new thing.
If entry fees could make his pockets swell,
you'd swear that ravenous poets and bardering
magpies at last the Pegasean nectar sing.

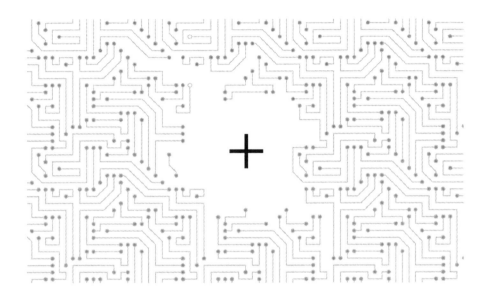

UPON NEWS OF THE IMPORTANT FOSSIL

Those human features on the apelike creature
may be a watershed in the long debate.
The breathless fossil bones, found in a cave
in South Africa, may be the best we have.
Australopithecenes, with mixed and matched
traits seen through the mists of an early watch.
It tells nothing of some grand, showy intent,
but I like to imagine for a moment:
its fleshly circuitry, its behavior,
a made thing fashioning tools, a *faber*.
Those rhapsodically primitive little tools
of sharp stone and adapted twig, of ruling
dilemma and method's first intimation.
It may have traveled close to upright, straight
in the cool of the day, but could not yet tear
itself from trees, not ready for firmer earth
always. It says something, to imagine all
remaining ahead, dizzy festival
of ozones, phonemes, green zones, iPhones,
charred craters of conscience, newer loneliness.
And better—the limbs from which it dangled
still visible yet, at obliquest angle.

BC PROSPECT

I fully expect one day we will be
all latex and circuitry, pointillisms
of data so minuscule as to make
a microchip seem like a beer coaster
or koozie, or other gadgetry
I fondly associate with the Eighties.

Sometimes you can catch a glimpse
of a possible dark future that sleek
intelligence will inhabit, and whatever
dominates there, possessing
a deftly fabricated sentience
as in any admirable masterwork,

may already be looking backward
toward us, hell-bent operational,
so optimistic in our supposedly
enlightened cultural moment.
It may be better later, but will
that lateness be invitational?

I beg of you, answer me that,
you harbormaster of pebbled shores.
Somewhere between Surrey
and the Vancouver Airport,
I discovered at slightly varying
heights the giraffe-necked arms

and shiny, metal-meshed baskets
of several extended cherry pickers
occupying a hardware-store parking lot,
looking scary, like an army of robots.
Collectively they looked like a nest
for a thing uncaring of what we've made.

TIMES SQUARE THE FIRST TIME

Four blocks north of here we lost everything:
modest fortunes gone, stunned by the hubbub
swirling as the cards blurred. *Follow the ace!*
Follow the ace! The band of seeming indigents
surrounded us, cheered, talked our wallets open.
My friend was given five twenty-dollar bills,
and he kept winning. Next hand, cards spun
in helix patterns. Horns punctuated their script.
We wanted more and—missed the hit. That was that.
They bled us dry before our first knowledge.
Dark Nativity scene, contrived for us!
As swiftly they vanished. I'm still astonished
(somehow beautiful, that brotherhood)
by their industry, perfect choreography.
But how tasty the breakfast begged at the diner.
How good the proud scar we shared, the square's
dazzling grin. We were humbled, hopeless, less dim,
made alive by that fevered welcome. We'd never
recover and so the shining city awoke
to us: mid-Missourians, three broke kings.

MY FAVORITE BOLLYWOOD FILM

It includes a suicide, but is handled funnily.
It's very earthy, sort of *c'est la vie*.
There's also robotics, ladders,
dorm-room pranks, and labor—
I mean a young woman who goes into labor—
a dramatic birth scene, and scootering.

Everything matters, and nothing.
It's about karma. The whole thing.
Some characters go crazy and are crazily
singing: prandial tomfoolery, and also cranial.
Themes keep expanding like manifest destinies,
like the odes of Hölderlin, or amended tax codes.

A thermos haunts the film, unopened in multiple scenes.
Soon a monsoon comes, can first be seen
blurring the coast. Its coming, I realize now,
must have been timed with most sensitive care
as some scary, humongous symbol
of the woman's water breaking.

What I haven't given yet is a good impression
of the sheer willy-nillyness of its offered world,
full of color if not comfort. All of those gods
with their many arms coming out of the woodwork.
It's a lot like the Greeks, methinks, this Indian
sensationalism: divinities capricious but fertile.

When the plot finally gets way out of hand,
with all the guests dusting the buffet for prints,
the director invokes a cinematic mercy rule,
or it could be called such, if what we meant in fact
were rules maintained by an airtight, steel-trap
system determined by the strictest, most relentless logic.

ABOUT YOUR DELIVERY-ROOM VIDEO ON YOUTUBE

The baby's head has barely crowned the canal
when today's parents perpetrate this scandal.
Maybe *omphalos* is overrated anyhow.
Instead, go with mom's face, red like a Roman candle.

POLAROID ELEGY

Gone now or nearly so, or now gone
retro and so more available now
than ever.

But let's maintain this one ruminative fiction
of long-gone vision, the years last seen:
air and light

and handheld conjuration like a funeral-
home fan. The salvaging of lives,
imperfectly.

Thus fully, beautifully human,
like that poem by Pilizaio
da Bologna,

who ventured that Adam's being made
in God's image and being capable
of sinning

meant that imperfection was intrinsic.
(The poet's own sins made him
an authority.)

Just so the grainy, faded talismans
of that age's mechanical eye,
emulated

now by digital graphics programs,
except that a single click deletes
all mishaps,

instead of bearing them unknowing into light
like thermometers needing resetting.
Awkward ones

make me weep the most. I think of the SX-70
in the hands of Walker Evans, his everyman's
scrutiny

so bittersweet, or Andy Warhol like a sentinel:
one in hand, taking portraits of people's
genitals,

holy disco sessions for posterior's sake,
while this guy's and that gal's pants rest
at the knees.

Most pleasing of all, yellowed snapshot in the sun
visor of my father's maroon Caprice
Classic,

company car from Mattingly's. One night another
driver swerved through thunderstorms, sent
us to the ditch.

Forty-five-degree angle, shaken, more alive
than ever. I have never remembered
that cherished shot

he kept always just inches from his temple.

WHICH ONE DAY WOULD YOU CHOOSE TO LIVE OVER AGAIN?

I really don't know, but I do know this:
decidedly not that day spent hanging out
with Lemmy Kilmister of Motörhead.
The way his sideburns reached forward to kiss
his mustache led to existential doubt,
not to mention how he thrust the dreadful
neck of his bass guitar against my ribs
repeatedly, like some rowdy hard-rock cherub.

FIRST APARTMENT NEAR ST. MARY'S

I recollect at last those first few weeks
on Beacon Street: broke newlyweds, we hid
our finite riches in a little room,
a basement studio whose cost seemed gruesome.
Fresh from Corpus Christi, you learned to speak
a northern language, talk of "quarters" wide-
mouthed like a Chowdahead's wicked idiom.
That strangeness resonates as echoed heirloom.

November then alive with many things,
we bundled up, explored the neighborhood.
The couple at the Busy Bee would bring
their frenzied fighting there, and Chinese food—
just half a block away! Some days we stood
at our door to mark the room's great reckoning.

OUR NOSTOS

So long ago (he says)
those newlywed days
of sex and budgets,

living off family's
nuptial gifts while
we, uplifted, spent only

our days working
in bookshops, long hours
in toy stores. Spent

those first winter
nights, on Beacon Street,
in Boston, with leaden,

love-tired limbs
lovely and unconcerned
with the self, at last,

at rest on the futon bed,
unselfconscious,
underneath the wedding

gift of Ralph Lauren's
plaid comforter,
and beneath our innocent

heads, the plaid shams
I'd never heard of. That bed
was like an island

orienting the one
room, oasis
to which the single flesh

nightly returned,
around which the studio
apartment spun,

not unlike in central
respects the old,
olive-tree-anchored,

rooted bed of Penelope
and Odysseus, in their
earlier, briefly

royal days. There, they
retired nightly for rest shared,
telling of a day's stories.

Those were the days
before the uproar
and the setting sail

and long, besetting war,
and afterward, the indefensibly
delayed return,

increasingly unexpected,
there to the shore
of that sea-steeped island.

How foolish, how
truly silly he was!
Unaware

or indifferent to the miles,
various coasts ahead,
he had no idea

that the brooch would soon
be long lost, sunk
in the sea or bottom

of the harbor.
May every husband's labor
be seen for the little

thing it is,
worthlessly distracting
or ever on the horizon,

while the shroud is woven
or unraveled
as the candle burns down.

By the time
it happened,
the pair had begun

to take the shape
of their crooked elders,
grey in their years,

heavy with the years
between them,
lost, awaiting

a coming mist
to move across them
like the gentlest of hands.

In that tiny room
near Kenmore Square
we too were living

through an early history
we would never grasp
again, never again.

Broke, learning the routes
to the T, we took our own
young, lusty royalty

so seriously, queen
and king of each other's
bodies, and they were

sweeter gifts by far,
dearer to us
than all the horses,

silver basins, lampstands,
all the assembled treasures
of Pylos, Sparta, Phaecia.

FOUND & LOST

A thought. A marmalade alley cat
whose photo's on the kiosk at the market.
A star-shaped chocolate. A tiny plaid
dress from my daughter's *Madeline* felt board.
This week's tenth pencil, fourteenth paper clip.
The phone number of him, who has found me
after eight years, who told me of another's
apparent suicide two years ago.
Two years of something. That other friend.
The remote control's battery cover.
Parking ticket whose fine is never lost,
but, unpaid, is out there somewhere, multiplying
on some computer in a darkened room.
A scarf. One glove. The merely cold weather.
The sense of escape that comes from years.
And you, O reader, if this apostrophe
by rhetorical trickery occupies
you here, or you it, so that you appear
in the present in this place, then perhaps
you are lost to me too, the no-show sought
in the crowded room. Or nearly so. Maybe
only nearly so.

IMPROBABLE RESCUE OF THE HEART

Receiving a good update, and good words
from you, sending dispatches from the front,
your overworked mother's life in Denver.

Most glad to hear your ever sensitive
capacity, ever expanding, for joy—
as with your rhapsodic soul in Gmail:

Glued to cnn.com right now
watching Chilean miners get rescued.
O! my heart!

And bless that heart. May its nerve be prophecy
against this one: scheduled muscle mainly,
the heart that bears its function, nothing more,

that circulates its weariness and gall,
deigns to be hauled around on daily errands.
What a tiny, bitter pump it can become.

They all need similar desolations,
don't you think so? The briefer the better?
But a condescension nevertheless,

plummet in darkness. Till a gracious, sent
drilling breaks the lining, makes a tomb mouth.
Every heart needs a season of forthcoming,

twenty minutes upward in a cylinder.
The world's goodwilled care meets it at the top,
and from the dusty opening the heart

emerges, once again steps blinkingly forth
into the blessed grove of patient living,
as the broad expanses brightly greet it.

And soon, as a kind of counterexplosion
that heals all, or seeming so, a thousand
flares of camera flashes telegraph one wish,

signal rare and never-dared-sought welcomes.
The heart's made steady, fed and blanketed,
surrounded by those other, besotted hearts,

their carriers. Some chose to write it all down
down there, but appreciate just the same
(irradiant now) the day's invisible stars.

RECOVERY, GULF COAST

—at Christmastide

Visiting in-laws outside Corpus Christi,
I feel whole again, healthy in swell weather,
silent in this deck chair near the mesquite.
Chicago and the snow seem far from here,
my hacking cough that fogged the windshield.
Calm prevails like sailboats off the balmy bay.
Not this place only, but because the everyday
recedes against the yard's edge. Then the children—!
They play behind me, where it laps the curb.
Buoyant in their running bodies, our two squeal
in sweaty chorus with the neighbor kids,
who all have lovely names: Celeste, Camille,
Chloe. Three graces: zealous, undisturbed.
Or heavenly virtues: trio fresh from hiding.

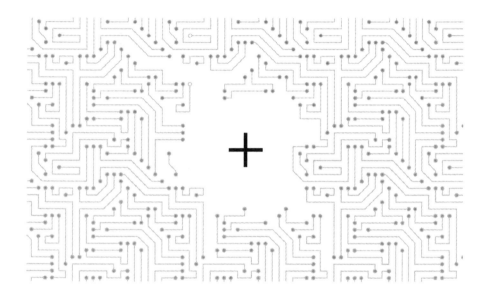

INSTRUCTION AND DELIGHT

I take a break and pace the small, dark rooms
of our apartment, sit in the ten-dollar chair
by the front door and think for a minute,
or gently turn on the bed lamp, lie down,
watch you spin unconsciously from the light.
Then to the bathroom where I comb my hair
for no good reason, none whatsoever.
Three cohabitant rooms: in each I hear
sounds of lovemaking, pitched above hypnotic
rhythms of beds or floor beams giving.
From the living room, operatic lovers
upstairs with their occasional squeals.
Beyond our bedroom the *Shazam!* of neighbors,
both of them curiously articulate,
loudly so. On the other side the almost
silent third pair, all incessant business
behind the medicine-chest mirror.
So late at night, and so much industry
dedicated to pleasure. And wisdom's there,
but distant in these hours. It is midnight,
it's a Friday. We're the early bird
and insomniac, you asleep and me,
wide-eyed and consummate, back at the desk.

I was young then but already with gusto
in my judgments: clearly a masterpiece,
and how dear to me still to find it so.
So many things wither in their unceasing
sameness, as we age beyond them and grow
too big in ourselves, that immediate release
of joyful encounter diminished as we go.
To watch again and not wince: a kind of peace.

And he, he makes it much easier of course.
"The wall's on fire!" A boy's eye for detail
lifts experience higher, followed by the force
of mutual mission because "Didn't I tell
you you better hold your light saber?" It's worse
to feel old—just bemusement at his swell
of enthusiasm, but our own excursus
must leave us satisfied. Each welcome's special.

Betrayal soon comes: empire and Boba Fett
threaten Lando Calrissian. The stress
of escape for some, for one the laser-lit
pit of reckoning, beneath the terraces
and greeting space, as antennas transmit
fates from temporary, cloud-capped Bespin.
Before it's done, "He's hanging by his feet!"
Then in the *Millennium Falcon*, wounds dressed,

he knows no better, thinks what's ahead is best.

ADULESCENTIA

Reading Belphoebe's ten-stanzaed blazon,
I calculate her many-angled loveliness,
fit it to you, or set you in the compass
of that able bouquet, if feebly, oh sweet one,

little one still. That doesn't mean those graces
will be unfamiliar. You should make them yours:
the skinny jeans and ring tones that restore
the glad self, and self-regard that replaces

those made or sold things. Guard your lovely heart,
full of talent, virtue lent, and weighing
more as it is shared. We're your one and only

no longer, though even when you're on your own
or lonely, waiting—there's no *away*, no way
but strongly companionate, even if apart.

AIRPORT UH-OH POEM

There must be something tumorlike
and ticking in the heart that makes me,
just off the jetway in Logan Airport,
darting from the gate and making my way,
react this way when I see the youngish
woman in the waiting room, just beyond
the guard's cordoned-off security line.
Her hand-markered cardboard sign
sits there beside her, thick with longing,
a tested patience to be rewarded soon.
Her body taut and charged with expectancy,
she could swoon any minute, thinking
of his arrival pending, that moment
unending in the memory about to be made
when he sees the sign she's made for him:
THE BEST BOYFRIEND EVER!
And I think how fickle or otherwise
unworthy he may be, how he may be
surprised by this, but not really in a good way,
how her enthusiasm just leaves me
fearful for her. You always choose
the enthusiasm you can live with,
obviously, but this feels troubling,
as if she had dropped an eggshell hope
into this guy's clumsy, unproven hands,
and thinking about it washes me up
on a pessimist's island: "They're doomed."

NO, YOU MISHEARD

I'm sorry that you thought I had said this was exciting.
Instead what I said in actuality was this—I'm exiting
now, disembarking from this entire scene between us
for some happily unknown as of yet port, under Venus
still if considerably distant from the many errands
we've been running. I'm happy too that it still stands
for something—that curvy, glittery star—ever the patron
overlooking lovers and their wandering barks and so on.
Now wait just a minute, I resent your calling me a coward,
resent it very much, although, yes, it's true, being a cowherd
remains my primary line of work, main source of my income.
So sorry we've come to cross-purposes, but better days are coming.
Of this, let us be mindful, and let us charitably sweep
our many minefields, which each prepared as the other slept.

SILENT COUPLE AT RIEVAULX ABBEY

The ruined choirs, of sky and stone,
inspired each of them alone.

The barest outlines of the nave
defined the problem none forgave.

On lancet windows' points they bled,
both anointed a Gilbert of Swineshead.

The smell of cut grass and clover
tried to tell them it was over.

The trail that crept out of the valley
would fail to keep them from their folly.

GEORGE CLOONEY

You gotta have a lot of *cojones*
to prank George Clooney, to phone him
late at night and say those outrageous things
about his young girlfriend, what's her name.
Just because she's from Las Vegas,
that doesn't mean she's a stripper, of course
it doesn't, please! She's just a cocktail waitress.
So what? His driver who's a cop traced it,
the number, back to a prepaid cell phone.
That was that. And imagine that—Clooney,
whom *Vanity Fair* last month called
The Last Actor in Hollywood, that guy
rudely awakened, middle of the night,
and those shocking words, the obscenities,
his anger like a punch in *Leatherheads.*
Earlier they had a motorcycle
accident, a miscommunication
at an intersection, common enough.
A lawsuit followed like a hungry child.
All year she wore an air cast, Red Carpet
here and there. They still smile, give an answer
numerous times, from head to talking head.
They hold hands as if they intend to last.
It isn't fair, this cost of being
one of us, even beautiful among us,
sad and perishable, often injured
and injurious. How he got the number,
why he swore at the movie star,
why they too must suffer ignominy
sometimes, and paparazzi—who's to say?
Bad enough to be hounded, ordinary
fury, but he shouldn't have to hear lies
about his girlfriend, who is young and strong
and will not have him around forever.

To feel the phlegm and spittle of success:
a little like Nim Chimpsky learning to sign,
enrolled in Columbia, more or less,
before downgraded as a Clever Hans
Effect, no worse or better than the math-inclined
trotter horse that toured Germany, nothing left
beyond the *Apple me eat /*
  Me more eat /
Give me eat / Drink me Nim / Tickle me Nim
play / and all the way to *Give orange give me*
eat orange me eat orange give me eat orange give
me you, which to some proved highly convincing,
after which retirement to Black Beauty Ranch,
where a heart attack darkened his studied mind;
and a little like that satin bowerbird
collecting tiny Legos, only blue ones,
from a backyard picnic table's half-built bridge.
He's obsessed with embellishing his nest:
= male-organ aesthetics, as with those cars
we joke of, red and sporty, meant to render
him more attractive to whichever looking bride
just winging by, alighting on the plastic.
    Likewise, every man is a vanity,
from the puffed-up vain who mirror themselves
to the painfully earnest ones, face flushed
with their causes. When asleep, their higher dreams
flash like klieg lights upon them. All will be well,
and within the swollen ego's laser point,
each self-anointed striver moves, self-deceiving,
irresistible, in the humbling words
of the psalmist, *like as it were a moth*
       fretting a garment.

JULY FOURTH, WITH VAMPIRES

The numbers were horrible, the poolside
a pleasure, the chlorinated
water bearable. I picture a multitude

pulsing through dark places
swarming on the healthy blood.
The arteries grew angular,

unknowing ones grew numb, carried on
the holiday. Bratwurst was sizzling
on the grill. The killing was worse

by being slow, as fat slowly clogged the blood.
Within the failing body,
good blood drains, triglycerides gather

to choke the life away.
Their numbers spike while inside
the fatal body bat wings unfold.

Protected from the sun,
these interior monsters howl,
full of grease, sated with sugars.

Our leisure, it becomes complicated, I said
to my younger self, not pale yet,
veins not yet brittle. My heart grew cold

beneath the midsummer sun.
Statins make their promise like a silver
stake through the heart, and yet

disease still settles with its monocle
and widow's peak, spreading
wide its black leather cape.

The day is sunny, the breath is easy,
but increasingly fat cells consume
the consumer, the patriotic one.

The teeth grow subtle with little cuts,
thicken the blood with vascular sickness.
The holiday is nearly done.

O CAPOLAVORO

More or less content in the uterine
green room, I nevertheless grew nervous,
kept practicing my lines.

Needing technique to be serious,
I auditioned for the role of a lifetime,
a barn burner, star turn, a fuss,

my face writ large, name lit up on Times
Square billboard. Instead, *Death played the lead.*
I toddled, spun the bottle, rhymed

and learned the art. Was way over my head
even with these bit parts.
Entering stage right, I soon could be heard

speaking as the Messenger, sounding smart,
those few lines as I declared the victor
or praised the dead's valorous hearts.

Gaining experience, I was the one they picked
to lament the dead queen,
report the young lovers' maledictions.

Now I'm most often seen
as the Third Servingman carrying a plate
in silhouette with a degorged aubergine.

My job is to serve that or pomegranates
(I don't refuse), or bring the duke a comb,
pillowed, bemuse him with shadowy wit.

Eventually I'll move downstage, become
a kind of costar. Hypocrite's destiny—!
To be the leading man, handsome,

assured, never at a loss for words, blessed
with wisdom, or at least *discrezione*.
Great cost, but I'm trying my best.

It's as if I'm meant for these lines I say,
role played consummately, as it's never been.
I'm rehearsing every day.

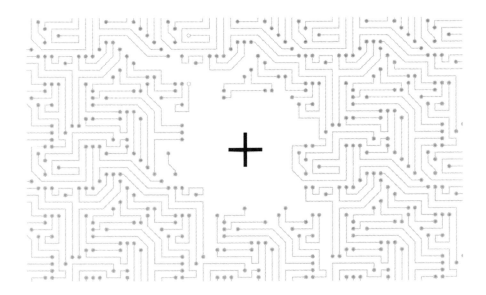

PSYCHOMACHIA

Call them either derricks or pumpjacks,
but never forget they are neither
gorging on obedience—severe rites
of incessant kneeling to bend away
or burn off their stains, their vices—nor,
at once determined and reckless,
jaw tightened and with slippers
flipped off nearby, with great commitment
blindly hungry, are they going down
on someone. That's simply what we
divided ones see, as the good and bad
angels dance and tangle on our shoulders.
One's a frail old man. One's a samurai.

THREE CITATIONS ON OUR NATURE

Too often to feel like Angelo
in Shakespeare's problem play,
to whom Isabella appeals, and rails
about proud man dressed in little briefs,
or rather "little brief authority."
Our glassy essence is the problem.
It plays fantastic tricks. Soon enough
all the angels turn to crybabies.
They laugh themselves beneath
themselves: less celestial, more splenetic.
Then there's Lakers small forward
Ron Artest, boarding the team bus
in his underwear, Looney Tunes
theme playing in the soundtrack
in his head. "Unique," once said
a teammate. Chagrin-maker, odd duck,
he's prone to improbable shots,
courtside fist fights. Is a goat
in the outhouse (his own words).
"He has a penchant for little things
tripping him up in the process,"
his coach says of Artest, a product
of the Queensbridge projects.
Human penchant, that is, "so he is kind
of dogged by his own nature."
Finally, Berryman's poet at eighty,
in "Eleven Addresses to the Lord":
"don't try to reconcile anything . . .
this is a damned strange world."
Nonetheless a world, according to
dear Berryman, hearing nothing
in "Thy kingdom come," nonetheless
a world still capable of awaiting
His prepared astonishments.

ELYSIUM

"The two in haste strode on down the dark paths
Over the space between, and neared the doors. . . .
Wider expanses of the high air endow
each vista with a wealth of light. . . ."

Unwished-for pivot in every journey—
the jet lifts off to shoot forth doubtless
then second guesses, draws back its engines,
sparks in nervous passengers that fear
refined by countless fairground videos,
airshow disasters seen on "real" TV,
fatal continuity of rise and fall.
I chose this seat and now must deal with it.
Beside me sits a black boy from Tupelo
who simply wants to know about my life,
each worthless fact in vast detail, as quick
as he can ask. His words should be a gift,
his anxiousness efface the traveler's mask.

Attendant barking how the baggage goes,
he looked abandoned, and I must have felt
momentarily fatherly, my own
daughter far from there. He sought reassurance:
this flight would be a snap, I prophesied.
As we taxied forward, we swapped our tales
of LA and Atlanta. He'd never been
but had some aunts in each, phantom cities
popping in his head. A.J. made adjustments
to his lap belt, held Cub Scout binoculars.
Glasses caught the gleam of the lamp above.
I wish we had a portable TV,
but it would probably not have cable, huh?

Now the turbo whir grows louder, seems to be
much like the overworked accoutrements
of a treasure hunter's prop plane, which caused
my heart to flicker *Raiders of the Lost Ark.*
Wow, it's really beautiful! says the boy,
surveying how the whitelit crop of stars
appears as shades amid the fields of Nashville
far below. How I want to be worthy,
a perfect witness of that speechless trance.
I manage only benign annoyance.
The day gone dark, night heavy already,
I lack the glad, attentive capital
his many questions give me credit for.

He soon looks bored with my reticence
and opens his book on classic Corvettes.
Two oatmeal cookies hidden in my jacket
would rather not be shared. Hungry, silent,
I am reading too, the latest volume
by a great poet I barely care for.
Expected to write about it, I'm struck
by the tiny benefits of literature:
were we suddenly to stall and plunge noseward,
to know I was holding *this* in my hands!
A guy should hold the best lines at those moments,
as when I saw an engine's case erupt,
aflame on a disinterested left wing,

some fifteen minutes out of Amsterdam.
A curse jerked me from *Crime and Punishment.*
The blast lit up my neighbor Pole,
his quiet, steady face a flash of gold,
temple wall where that falling boy was absent.
When stuttering pilots poured tons of fuel
into the North Sea's silver anodyne,
a kind of libation for the deep pool,
only the old words stayed believable,

not this new stuff. A.J.'s had enough of cars
by now, asks me how to find the bathroom.
The engine strife begins to subside, softer,
converting our ascent to something safer.

Halfway home, and as my seatmate pees
at thirty thousand feet for the first time,
sleep casts his questions as numberless leaves.
I picture Providence, my thoughtful friends
who wait there, and my family farther off,
apartment quieted by sleep's descent.
My little girl's bedroom hums in darkness,
pipes rattle, and he passes over me,
clumsily, marvels at the bathroom. I
imagine walking down the drafty jetway,
cold air caught in the whitewashed paneling,
through a better gate absent of falsehoods,
random landmark for any landed dream.

SONNET

—after Dante

Alan, I wish that you and Mark and I
were swept up in some lottery's happy net
to first-class seats. (Or—why not?—corporate jet.)
No harassing fortune as we sailed the sky.

We'd hear some bluegrass at the Grisly Pear,
see Rylance on Broadway, either in *La Bête*
or storming Rooster in *Jerusalem*—all set.
Together in wit, we'd wish for more days shared.

Anise, Teri, and Mary would show eventually,
whose cherished names appear far higher than ours
in the Book of Life, and other lists besides.

In Bryant Park we'd speak of love for hours,
always love. They'd be as psyched, our three brides,
as I believe the three of us would be.

SUMMER TEACHING AT AN OXFORD COLLEGE

We spent those seven weeks in Trenaman House,
or let's call it what it was: dormitory.
And there were my Vans, and there was your blouse
flung across the chair, tossed along the floor.
To have our lives collapsed within that room
like cardboard eaten by a thunderstorm—
it simplified our love and pushed the tomb
away, with its grey-haired, mortgaged comfort.
We shortly came to cherish those four plain walls
containing the banalities that fed us:
ginger biscuits, fruit snuck from the dining hall,
teapot whose heating rods were almost dead.
Quizzes graded, a gladder business called,
those comic gymnast's stunts on your twin bed.

TO DAVID HOOKER

I can't believe there may yet be
another world where we'll sit next year
and share our work with each other,
say, a tufa mound in the Umbrian sun.
You can be Israel Idonije; I'll be Peanut Tillman.
Or you be Julius Peppers and I'll be
Devin Aromashodu. Neither
you nor I will be Pierre Garçon,
but the Holy Ghost will still look on,
beaming from the harvest moon,
beaming at us awkward men, side-hugging
as we leave the Duomo or watching
amber-colored, polyester resin
settle on the single, oversized leaves
of your book carved for Epiphany.
Shall we be really gone? And gain the studio
I glimpsed in my youth? If the moon,
when it rises tonight, is empty—
no worries, then: that's a good sign,
meaning "Fill again the earthenware mugs,
top them off, as a rented houseboat
drifts along the current, windows open,
Carolina spring, and others watch us
from the smoking bank spin ever
so slowly in the brown waters of Catawba."

DISCUSSING SOCIAL MEDIA WITH HER

Driving all day, tooling
across the whole state of Pennsylvania,
now rolling in and cooling
before the hotel TV—a congressman

disgraced and everywhere
for sexting coeds, tweeting buffed photos:
him in his underwear,
or in the buff. We say, oh dear, oh no,

to hear of anyone
exposed so, suffering that kind of fall.
The news is almost done.
"Wouldn't happen to Clooney, not at all,"

she says upon learning
the actor doesn't Facebook, never tweets.
He's got no time to burn,
I say. Each day he cruises narrow streets

in sun-clad Perugia
surrounded by friends on motorcycles:
glad excursions, deluge
of wine, genuine living. No sickles

bent or many hours spent
before a screen, virtually capable.
She added urgently
between commercials: "Don't forget hot babes."

BEGINNING OF AN ELEGY, WITH IPAD

"Would you keep an eye on my little machine
for me?" he said as he rose, made his way
slowly to the men's room, where he would lean
against the wall, resume negotiations, obey

the aging bladder further burdened now
by hostile treatments. He posts under deadline.
His updated, upgraded iPad waits—wow!—sturdy
and sleek, its neoprene sleeve left behind

the chair on the ledge. Small wetsuit. Tiny shroud.
Its screen does not distract or speak, or not much:
reflects (a comfort?) cortegelike drifts of clouds
where just before a keyboard held his touch.

AT A CABIN NEAR BARRONVALE BRIDGE

I joked that hand-and-foot canasta
sounds a lot like foot-and-mouth disease.
Everyone was displeased,
returned to their game.
I became, such as I was, more myself,
feeling like Edgar Kaufmann or another dynast.
Everything lately is fresh to the taste.

Sitting in a chaise longue, reading
Herodotus. All day off, and still here.
I stayed on the cheerful
porch alone, while the rest
all the more earnestly played at their cards,
hoarding red threes inside. The trees seemed to bleed
as summer's thunderstorm intensified.

The Facebook poll you told me about,
eating pizza for breakfast—good or bad?,
is blessedly faded
from my attention now,
or is about to be. Now is the season
for seeing clearly again, the eyes shouting
or undergoing something tantamount

to new life for senses wasted away.
Today, I grew enamored with the sound
of water rebounding
off rocks in the creek
thickening beneath me because of the storm,
forming a haven, near where Fall Run gives way
to Laurel Hill. Tonight, I feel confluential, swaying.

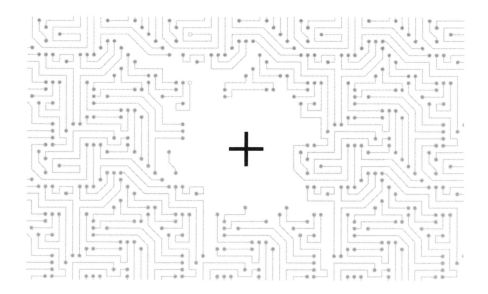

ARTES LIBERALES

"The miserable servitude
of the spirit"
is not exactly how one wants to hear it:
that's just plain rude.

Yet Augustine, I suppose,
knew a thing or two
of everything one must do
to grow out of requisite imbroglios,

to grow out of your own
heart, or at best,
to enter the contest
imparting a different throne

or emancipated alter
ego. Let go the facts
wearing their cataracts
or pirate's patch of faults,

swelling shortcomings. Instead,
raise the mind's eye
to vaulted ceilings high
overhead, as Hippo's bishop said,

and forgo all carnal acts
of reading (though honest ones
would say that sure sounds fun).
Pay the mental luxury tax.

And by so doing, cultivate
a heart vivified.
Only the bland or snide
or blinded conflate

or substitute the sign
for thing, and therefore keep
failing to bite through or drink deep.
It's a thin line,

and yet a vast chasm as well,
to shift from our blunt
meth-head spasms to wisdom's font
and dwell

within a cedared house there.
Ambiguity, causing pain,
spurs the bludgeoned reader big with chains
and requires no little care.

MEMENTO MORI, WITH SUMMER FAIR

On the message board, Theosofest poster
for next week's fair. It touts "The Influence
of Our Future" and other sessions, free of cost.
The past signs off on us with signatures
either opulent or ruinous. But whence
our lives from here on out? There is no cure,
meant narrowly, and so of course the future
haunts our decaying hearts. If we stray
past immediate, a single holocaust
is waiting for us all. It makes one pensive.
It hunts us, or we're driven on our own
by every second—and glad ones, even those—
toward some mortal corner, baleful sixth sense
beyond the senses, hard and logical way.
Is that what the sunny poster means to say?
I confess, I want a peace that overflows
the formula, carried to the final figure.
Let's anticipate instead a dark scene,
fair enough, but also one that's somehow swaying
in front of us, inviting from where we've been
to some place fully realized, more serene.
Did I mention it's so inviting, so assured?
Imagine walking around in a kind of relay
of the wise, among a host of cheerful tonsures.
I think of the "second naïveté"
of Paul Ricœur, accepting, safely arrived,
anchored just off the outer banks of our lives.
We'll be contrite, sufficient in our knowing,
self-left in good ways. Emboldened, we'll lower
the rope, receptive to the motions, that most
welcomed of internal states once given
to comfort Adam, late in *Paradise Lost*.

REQUEST OVERHEARD ON A CAR RADIO

The boy who calls on the phone line
requests our prayers for a girl he knows
from youth group, and whose world
is dissolving as her love goes blind.
Her mother, as he tells the show,
"is having cancer"—someone's old-
world grandfather might have said it so.
And fondly I recall a friend fresh
from marrying his love in Messina,
whose father-in-law had said, "They wish,
these two, to conjugate," and toasted
the pair joyously. But the boy's message?
It resembles the way we'd say a host
is expecting (you're invited to the shower)
or else is having a friend to supper,
an invitation maybe sent
in chiseled verse of Roman epigram.
Yet the earnest point is not lost.
The entreaty's cause remains the same
whether as rescue or troubled begging
for one declining, only days to go.

There comes a knowledge beyond the knowing,
comprehending growing up,
or must, if we're to reckon the cost.
A common humbling grinds the bones
(and I mean everyone's bones, eventually)
or rather, if the phrasing can try better—
lightly done yet not swooning in subterfuge—
it stops the frugal trials of increasing aging,
so says the Paul's Cross preacher, time of plague.
Such comeuppances will cease the flagging.
Tell me, though, if this feels true?
And so the boy seeks remedy, or refuge.

MEDITATION ON "IN MEMORIAM"

Not "is survived by," that gravely passive voice
to deactivate the dead, but "He leaves his wife
of fifty years, Constance," as if the journey
were his to determine, and compared with this life
the more important thing. There is no choice,
but there may be a setting forth, a way with key
in hand to unlock some admittedly unknown
door or portal. In other words, maybe he's busy,
careless of the cherished days left behind (below?)
and in such a departure neither bed-ridden nor dizzy
nor undignified, he leaves a little of his leaving
so that it's hers, too, making the event hardly
more than errand, if indeed his faculties were sturdy:
"leaves," she almost believes, will carry off her grieving.

THE STATE WE'RE IN

Across the crowded, sunlit room
the bald man in the running suit
calculates how hard the fall will be.
"We'll sell the house, no going out.
We'll depend on one another more.
It's going to be good for us."
So the job's gone. Bankruptcy looms.
So what? he says. "It's reality,
and we're around to live through it."

It could become about me now:
analogous indictment burnt
not in flesh, but in more tender
advantages of the spirit.
How the numbers accumulate—
so many blessings and negligence,
or efforts bargaining for grace.
There must be some remarkable
fountain, for the bonded to drink from.

Him? This guy's numbers are long gone,
and he seems lighter. Is it, "angel—?"
No, *ankle* wings. Like Mercury's,
bossier messenger, shrewd god
for rogues and cattle thieves, broker
for the foreclosed dead in Hades.
Not to obsess on assets lost
nor drink too fast from Bethesda:
gratitude's middle road, at least.

THE TREE FELLED, THE TREE RAISED

When you worked as a forester once, once
another who worked alongside you lost
a hand, and it fell to you—the one
who had to "tie it up." Perhaps that's why
Washington's wilderness rarely fills your poetry.
Discretion's chainsaw clear-cuts what is most costly.

Then Leslie weighed in with her sweet expertise
on how a logger's life ought not to be idealized,
and how even the saw allows for the trees
it's just about to bring down, eliminated
from Alaskan landscape. This koan is like bait:
hooked, I contemplate destruction's subtle sizes.

The changes and chances of this mortal life
are cries to call the soul back home again.
At least I like the way that sounds, even if
the little tree house of the body is all
we really know, wounds and pine knots, as squalls
pound the limbs in which the bare, beamed room is contained.

Yesterday a friend's mother paid a visit
to our church, and by the creed we developed
a partnership: bulletin between our heads.
For her, it was possibly (why pretend?)
a way forward, readying for the end.
"Begotten," as I heard her say, "and not made up."

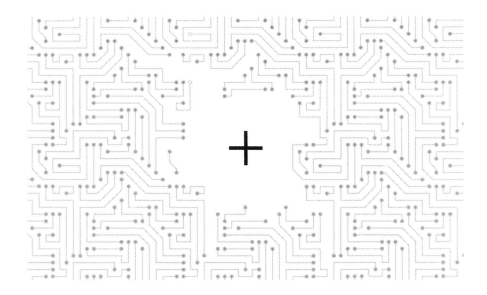

HAPPINESS, CAROLINA HIGHWAY

I tried to sing falsetto
amid the pine and palmetto.
I had a golden god's bravado,
made bold by my Eldorado.

QUIET *ARS POETICA*

I have always been heartened
by the varying degrees the art
bends for us, the ways it sings
forth like a jolly itinerant begging
through far domains of prayer,
curse, and oath. It's always there
staring out through the words'
disguises, dolled up in curlers,
wearing a ski mask or sackcloth,
strategizing to mean otherwise.
Sometimes they assault the skies,
manufacture tears with rain dances.
Sometimes they forgo all nuance
for the sake of saying it clearly,
their tiny truth a gift left in the ear.
Thus this welcomed art views us
as through a dome's oculus.
I have always been heartened
by the ways by which this art
will say the most beautiful things,
build temples of sadness hanging
nearly off the edge of a precipice.
This thoughtful art brings a peace,
charts a course through internet
attachments forwarded when better
days have ceased, when the mind
begins to smell moldy, feel menial,
needs a cane or a kind of cannabis.
At least it waves peace's banner
for those sensible enough to take
it all in small doses. For saucy jacks
who know no better, who treat it
so seriously, for so long, entreating

the art's powers to sing a little
more strongly amid mostly belittled
circumstances, meaning the rest
of the world, let them do their best
to make a go of it, act grown up
as already they dance, swing, skip,
driven by engines of ingenuity
through fields of the mad and free.

ALTERNATIVE TITLES FOR THE BOOK YOU ARE HOLDING IN YOUR HANDS

Aqua Vitae
Afternoon Pilgrims
Afternoon, Pilgrims
Angel's Share, The
Answerless
Apostle of Markets
Bangers & Mash
Book of Various Expenses
Bread of Idleness
Café Padre
Caged Wisdom
Cortegiano's Piano, Il
Courier of Spirits, The
Damage Per Second
Data Mime
Development of Qualities, The
Discrete Witnesses
Divinitie & Drincke
Duende's Endnotes
Duke of Chicagoland, The
Dynamic Positioning System
Echo-Criticism
Eel Fritters
Entreatable
Eurhythmy
Fall Run Road
Fulfillment Center
Google & Prayer
Googled Prayer
Gravel Angel
Heather & Fescue
Heaven Go Easy on Me
Hope for Creatures
House of Merchandize

Idiot Savant
Inside Voice
Is It Me, or Does It Smell Like Cat Butt In Here?
Jaw Harp
Jehoshaphat's Bath Mat
Light Box
Magnificent Dummy
Maximum Selfie
Melt Rate
Middle Voice, The
Meaner Praises
Music Bureau
Music in the Air
Of Rates and Bubbles
Overdog
Portions for the Maidens
Prayer & Google
Prayerful Googling
Shadow Cabinet
Shadow Work
Schmale Bandits
Sore & Strong
Storm Surge
Sub-Acute
Summer's Russet Cheek
Sweet the Art
The Ticklish Months
Three-Nerved Leaf
Time
Tsipouro Phone Booth
Thunder Snow
Updraft
Uptick
Venture Capital
Venus in Transit
Vocalities
Wearable Robot
Wind Farm

LEXICAL REVERIE

Now say "public library" three times fast
and feel your voice give corners to the air.
Now hear the funny names my son has carried:
Boots and Gusto, Bips and Bixby, Mr. Sassafras

or Picklefeather—try that one on for size.
The skies in our heads are bright with characters,
song's constellations, linguistic cataract.
Steadily hewn, honed by angel tongues, words realize.

SPATULAMANTIC

"Fine, just go ahead and take the spatula
yourself," she said, making the grease
splatter, storming from the kitchen.
I was majorly in my manic phase then,
and, gimlet-eyed, was seeking some relief
from *mater scapulitis* and the fistula
I was constantly nursing, like raw grief
that kept spreading all over the skin,
roving here and there in traditional ways.
At that very moment the divination
hit me, speaking to me from the cattle
entrails sizzling on the stove top,
as I worked the spatula back and forth.
I knew then there was nothing to say,
nor would be, nor anything worthy
left between us. Our mouths never opened
at dinner that night (except when we
devoured the entrails). I could still see
deep into the future: she like an old,
fierce temple priestess, holding her own
beastly clavicle still smoking as offering,
forever giving me the cold shoulder,
as if I were the worst kind of phony
always stuck on a cell phone, or as if
I were standing there but hardly heard,
barely overheard even, yelling absurdly,
seen merely as some stuttering centurion.

ON LEONARDO'S "FIGURES TO REPRESENT LABOR"

Their various tasks make a human tower
rising out of the notebook bottom, or a mound
from which the pivotal figure has pulled
a gnarled, root-girdled stump. He's dragging it
somewhere not seen, body in counterangle,
anchored leg, lungs heavy with silent grunts.
The one below him might be sighing as
he drops his hoe once more forward. Dark lines
on his inner thigh stand for shadow,
suggest the artist's hand when it quickens,
technically sure of its chiaroscuro.
Framing them, several vessel carriers
attempt their different means of transport—hip,
arm, or shoulder—whatever holds up longest;
a lone, staffed one like ferryless Charon;
a top aggressive pair that prefigure
two demons from Doré. No activity
exists, or else does but clearly stays there.
Thus no thought, no form becoming something more.
Promise of motion only. Yet one glimpse
supplies an energy, fire inside the leaden pose,
while repose is made articulate by each
mid-deed, modestly everlasting.

AVERY DA VINCI, OUR LADY OF THE WESTERN SUBURBS

In the upper room that is her bedroom,
she spends her sick day, part fevered, part bored.
It's hard to remember that you're adored
by those who love you when you're thirteen. Life's doomed,

or at least it's gloomily slow for her today,
already grounded before she grew ill.
So she reads her fill of graphic novels
sent by a kind friend from my grad school days,

who knew her as a toddler, saw a glimmer
of vision in her doodled pictures even then.
Better to serve the Sforzas of Milan
than be a teen, painting by the body's timer.

Upstairs, she works with daring on her art
assignment, which is to adapt a given
masterpiece. She's transforming da Vinci's
Last Supper into a full-blown birthday party,

leaving the apostles to rave with the best.
I love her subversive genius in the pious
suburbs, fancy it a legacy. (I'm biased.)
Grant her happiness, O Lord, and give her rest.

MISSIVE

—found on a migrant worker in the barrens of southern Arizona

Today I am thinking
about all that I have lost
and why you are not close
to me. The mountains
are difficult to cross.

ON STANLEY SPENCER'S *TRAVOYS ARRIVING WITH WOUNDED*
AT A DRESSING-STATION

"I can draw better than Picasso."

After the Bulgarian Armistice,
newly back in Cookham and malarial,
he began the painting in the unheated,
abandoned stable standing behind Moor Hall.
"The ice house," he called it, a rather far cry
from the Greek port of Salonika, where he landed
to join the Macedonian front line
and experience in person the theater of war
following the disaster of Gallipoli.
He rode in ration oxcarts through the valley
and met the stretcher bearers up a ravine,
as the bivouac lines stood out from landscapes
reminding him of childhood biblical scenes.
Somehow he felt a "spiritual peace" amid the trenches
and churches skeletal from prior Balkan wars.
Once demobilized, he continued to carry
around the memory of a mountain range
dividing Bulgaria from Greece, and heard
again the jingle and squeak of mules' harnesses,
or clanging sounds of steel poles against rocks.

Which brings us finally to those wounded soldiers.
The perspective is what's most noticeable,
aerial orientation that contemplates
the healthy as they treat the other ones,
their faces concealed by mosquito netting.
And all this witnessed, taken in, from above,
from an almost proximate God's-eye view
(what does that mean?) if God had ever deigned
to descend so low and show so much
as any interest. That glimpse as from an atoll

grips the viewer, as do accumulated thistle
and the milky veins upon the holly leaves
in the painting's bottom corner, sharp and bright
like sea urchins set to swallow the setting.
We view a row of travoys, queued up outside
a little, disused church where urgency
has turned it into an operating theater.
The golden light by which the surgeons work
seems nearly transfigurative. But first we look
upon those wounded ones fatefully positioned there.
They are covered in wool blankets, folded over.
One's foot starkly peeks out from a blanket.
One's in the fetal position, alone and afloat
in an indifferent universe. Another's compressed
to half his size, as if trying to achieve a vanishing.
As if their present lives were nothing so much
as the sum of the wheelless wheelbarrows
that carried them, the mules that led them,
the medical orderlies holding up the travoys
behind them. *Travoys*, whose Latin root means
"an instrument of torture," like Tyburn's traitors
led on a rail past London's city limits,
out to the gallows and the vivisections.
I suspect the wounded could imagine it
better than before, the acute reality
of emboweling by whatsoever means
modern or early modern. The four mules
stand above the foreshortened wounded,
excessively curious, black with their rumps
facing us, and they with their cute, pert ears
could be merely seated in front of us,
in stadium seating inside a cineplex.

They are firsthand spectators of the miracles
occurring there or not, there at the makeshift
dressing station at Smol, the church transformed,
beyond the shells' bombardment and the fallen
battalion outside the walls of Kalinova.

74

Through a window more enlarged than one would guess
(divider between windows recently removed),
the mules observe an operation in progress.
The patient is enjoying his withdrawal,
his unmistakable change of atmosphere,
a "species of peace" according to the artist,
not terrible nor sordid, but with a grandeur.
Spiritual ascendancy dwarfs the artillery
as the backed-up, lined-up wounded wait
calmly, their pain having become a small thing.
They belong to a different world like Christ
on the Cross, he says, and those tending them
are disciples of an undesiring kind,
inserting peace in the war's clenched face.
The wounded: separate groups of nebulae
or conforming saints enthroned, stretcher handles
shining like heavenly instruments or ornaments
in an antique Orthodox altarpiece.
If there were angels, they would float reassuringly
near these men within currents of morphine.
But there are no angels here, although two
of the wounded speak of growing cabbages.
No canopy, providing shade for the window,
is needed any longer at this hour, among shadows
and summer moonlight. Within, the iconostasis
maintains its holiness. The mules' ears point
toward that boundless light and the magilike
encounter happening there, resplendent
work of surgery performed on the altar table.
Paraffin or naphtha lamps illuminate
the kill floor, where the injured are made
capable again, or relinquished forever.

Watching, too, the service corps's mule drivers
stand beside their burden-bearing charges
holding riding whips, or with rifles in hand.
Farther off an ambulance, also mule-drawn,
awaits its load, is destined for the Casualty

Clearing Station or a hospital ship
to Alexandria if some damaged travelers
are fortunate in their being so massively broken.
The dead will be more easily buried nearby,
outside of the frame of Spencer's painting.
Within the painting, though, its entire world
becomes a refuge, is imbued with something
homely and constructive. A final watcher
is a soldier not only living but standing
also, supposing himself transcendent
even as he watches with his arm in a sling
the farthest from the window's unearthly light.
He is the one closest to us, though,
most visible to us. At this moment he feels
what it really feels like when a God falls.

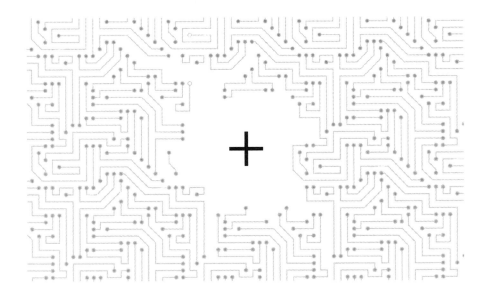

FROM A PLANE WINDOW WEST OF SAN DIEGO

"the intermediate somewhat between a thought and a thing"
—Samuel Taylor Coleridge

Pillar of fire that churns the Pacific?
Triton's shoulder surfacing? No, any old spine
descends, confuses vision and fuselage
out my wing-seat window.

Along that spine a gradual, loveless dimming.
And where it dims the water's surface teems,
as brushed with caustic paste, or rip-muscled purl
of thinnest cast armor.

Only the one thing can look just so like that.
No everyday world, no tray of gnarled receipts
or cup of cold tea. No peanut dust on sleeve.
Against this sad tableau

sparks the webwork of darker rivulets
in that film, or corridors of birds almost,
squawking and voluminous fluttering,
fluttering their brilliant

ceaselessness of wings. Conjured now, the coast
brings bowed bridge rising. We pass Mission Bay's
wooden roller coaster and drop lower over
the cockled rooftop shells.

GOOD NIGHT

I love you, Love, I usually whispered
as she slept there, soon to rise
in two hours, her back facing me
as I turned off the reading light
shining like a miner's lantern. For me,
insomnia again and finally the emptied,
scorched end of this extended day.
It was ours together, we realized,
and overly costly, like everything we kept.
In the room's dark, from the window
above the bed I stood beside, already
a thinning, a hint, a predawn expectation.
I noticed two plastic white lawn chairs,
solemn and on guard, guarding each side
of the sliding doors of the woodshed,
a hermitage in the tiny lot's corner.
The pale, glowing chairs became two ghosts,
separate and steadfast, still depressive
even at the height of their afterlives.

THE OPPOSITE OF "LOV"

My best of beloveds, better than Amaryllis
or Phyllis or whoever else old verse has praised,
I would like to rephrase this habit of mine
of gazing your way with profusions of words
and say here simply that I did not mean it
when in today's earlier message, too quickly sent,
I wrote "Lov, Brett" as if it were afterthought,
thought sloppily or half held, as if it didn't foretell
and fill in everything fiery that keeps you brightening
around me, unforgettable in these marshland days.
Italians say it with an "s" but, naïve or native, let's say
"exquisite" with its redundant "e," and from that word,
fitting as it is, I commit love's felony and complete
my prior fragmentary valediction. I do this all for you,
so that my "Lov" and love might reach you yet
across the brightly cold servers and the more human
networks besides, that it might still catch your eye,
its servant's confidence regained and serious again.
Wearing its armband, it calls for you in its fullness.

FOR A YOUNG SOFTWARE DESIGNER, WHO NEVER SLEEPS

My history is to find the next big thing early.
> —Mitch Kapor, founder of Lotus Development Corp.

Sovereign, insofar as you manage
to strengthen those inventions that define
our age and leave it slightly less savage.
Technology class spawned thoughts of space pods,
world windows with Galactica designs,
not the strange language of command and code.

In the beginning code made the hours fly.
Then our interest crashed. Slow in its routine
and not flashy, these TRS-80s,
no kaleidoscope colors, but two-tone
and bare, lime-green cursor on a lead screen.
It took seven steps to add 3 + 1.

Maybe we were modern already, anointed
ones annoyed by this huge calculator's
true function: to leave us disappointed,
pointing beyond itself, wired medium,
relic spurring on its next creators,
modest vision of some mastery to come.

LOOKING BACK ON THE ERA OF YOUTUBE

By this means, they tried to make themselves immortal,
the scroll of their days and silly jokes unrolling digitally,

the flickering video rolling ever onward tirelessly
recording, continuously on as they uploaded incessantly,

clicking on phone or tablet, as if to make penny offerings
to the great god they had raised to make themselves laugh.

But in the end, these efforts were bereft of benefit, no oath
of wisdom there—fit only for the entertainments of others.

These little testaments they left became fools' coercions:
ghost screens, constant shame, meat aglow for bullying diversions.

ON THE WAY TO WHERE WE'RE GOING

I'm trying to repress the email message
my mother sent me, about thirteen ways
to measure the length of your life remaining,
thoughtfully tallied by Northwestern Mutual.
Thank you, O actuarial angels,
with your handfuls of gravel aimed at me.
I'm blocking it out now with my eyes closed,
behind the wheel at the corner of Providence
and Stadium, as if I currently idled
at my future's gladiatorial crossroads.
It is surprisingly pleasing when I realize
that, even with closed eyes, I can sense when the light
turns from red to green, can feel the lightening
upon my veiled yet serviceable perception
signaling all-clear and therefore urging me forward.

Where shall we go? How best to go about
those minimal efforts at comfort, at least?
Which avenue eventually will reveal itself,
disclosed behind this or that turn up ahead?
Every destination offers a kind of sanctuary
like a coupon, good for stopping there permanently,
suitable endgame, peace everlasting. Would that it were so.
Instead we find ourselves playing bit parts
in a mind-game film, unsure what's coming or going.
It turned out to be a pit stop after all,
and all the while above us the Messerschmitts
and Spitfires were dancing their duck-and-covers
overhead, continuing their routines.

Still awaiting us out there is the Villa
Palmieri with its surgically cared-for lawns,
Mannerist hedge sculptures, and labyrinthine
gardens whose visitors are required to carry

SOS flares for leisurely emergencies,
sudden disorientations most common
among the one percent. It is no true conclusion,
of that make no mistake, but is desirable
as what we might as well call a *hortus conclusus*,
a spot perhaps reachable for us for days
of storytelling or any other diversion
or submission to wisdom as the palazzo's
dwellers wait out the plague in relative health.
It is there, or a place roughly approximate to there,
where we will reminisce about the old ways,
mull over the glimpsed thrills of greater things
to come, and dream, with eyes wide open
and set within the vessels of our waking selves,
of ever more intricate schemes, extravagant rescues.

ON THE NUMBNESS THAT WILL BE OUR FUTURE

And then the weather turned cold and never got better,
and we were forced to wear our sweaters later and later,
at high school graduations, mid-June in Key West, these bright
commencements of the brightest, where shivering we sat,
surveyors of risers in our puffy vests. We would have cheered
had we not been holding our mittens, or holding the white
elastic that held them, tenderly permanent equipoise of decay
and perseverance. On most days we were wind-bitten, chapped.
Soon we sought maps to release us from unseasonal fronts,
which became constant, sans season. We took our winnings and spanned
the round world's four corners for white sands and comfort, but no
matter: to no avail. Even the grand beaches failed to please us
then, in those final days, even the blazing views of Australia's
Great Ocean Road were rendered with wind-chilled sameness,
Apollo Bay and Cape Otway just another Siberia more or less,
and we visitors who had so hoped for improvement, increased
vision and lifting temperatures, or at least inhabitable encampments
displaying vistas more welcoming, we too were growing ever more
forlorn, cut to the very bone by continually plummeting cold.
It kept expanding across the old world and new. By the new year
of the last year, we stood on the shore, backs to fires,
to ponder the Southern Ocean, and wonder if it were not
some great arbiter of our unwished-for, possibly merited fate.
We rubbed these thoughts together for it was all we had left,
like the mind's final, desperate kindling. Then our hands turned black-blue
and hope went cold, as our hair filled with salt and frost and fear.

PASSING THOUGHT ON APOCALYPSE

You may be in robe and curlers when it comes,
its big-time sparklers rousing us toward bomb shelters.

Those may be manifest signs of a kingdom
newly at hand, and not the helter-skelter

robbing of the present, benighted, made numb
by all you thought you knew, an infested belt.

The word suggests a curtain ripped behind the tombs,
emergent steps of something mighty. The rest, melting.

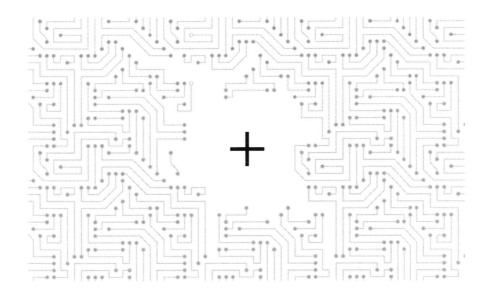

HORATIAN VALEDICTION

Reader, here is no know-nothing
muddlemouth grinning till his time's up,
    nor this month's charismatic hotshot—
        let's be glad for that.
Nor is it time for deeper, troubled things,
    the heaviness of swollen hands
that knit our sweaters, or underfed
teenagers who look like my six-year-old,
sweet in his warm bed.
                Shall I go on, then, or end it?

It's not even an occasion for lyrical
greatness (who can bear or hear it?), or honoring
the slain and scars of veterans
        (how to sustain it?) or excursions
on hermeneutical wings along the Word.
Or less estimable, more complicated forms
                of happiness:
breathless days when we became better
      than ourselves,
           as if awaking from a dream.

Let other songs bless or curse with big decibels.
I leave this business, such as it is,
to higher-minded poets or tireless annalists.

I sing simply of Love, of grace, and those graces
who are your friends, warm with life and giving
        you grief, playfully—these late evenings in December.
And I sing of such beautiful people, even closer,
safe and asleep nearby, here and there, her
           and her and him, so pleasing
and peace be with them,
and you too, Reader, you too.

ACKNOWLEDGMENTS

I would like to acknowledge the support of editors and staff at the following publications, where some of these poems first appeared (sometimes with slightly different titles or lines):

Anglican Theological Review: "The Tree Felled, the Tree Raised"

Arion: "Contra Belly," "Our Nostos"

Baltimore Review: "On the Numbness That Will Be Our Future"

Books & Culture: "My Favorite Bollywood Film," "Three Citations on Our Nature"

The Christian Century: "Horatian Valediction," "Lexical Reverie"

The City: "*Adulescentia*," "For a Young Software Designer, Who Never Sleeps," "Recovery, Gulf Coast"

The Common: "First Apartment Near St. Mary's"

4Humanities: "Artes Liberales"

Letters: "Avery da Vinci, Our Lady of the Western Suburbs"

Levure littéraire: "Happiness, Carolina Highway," "*Memento Mori*, with Summer Fair"

Liturgical Credo: "Request Overheard on a Car Radio"

The New Criterion: "Airport Uh-Oh Poem"

Pleiades: "From a Plane Window West of San Diego"

Poor Yorick: "On Leonardo's 'Figures to Represent Labor' "

The Seattle Review: "Found & Lost," "The State We're In"

Second Nature: "Looking Back on the Era of YouTube"

Shenandoah: "Meditation on 'In Memoriam' "

Sin Fronteras / Writers Without Borders: "Missive"

Subtropics: "Psychomachia"

Technoculture: "Polaroid Elegy"

The Yale Review: "BC Prospect"

"Recovery, Gulf Coast" also appeared in the anthology *The Gulf Stream: Poems of the Gulf Coast.*

"On the Numbness That Will Be Our Future" was awarded the 2014 *Baltimore Review* Poetry Prize.

Grants from the G. W. Aldeen Memorial Fund and the Alumni Fund at Wheaton College have supported the writing of this book. An Individual Artist Award from the Illinois Arts Council has been similarly supportive. A Howard Nemerov Scholarship made possible my participation in the Sewanee Writers Conference; it was very much worth the wait. Residencies at the Studio for Art, Faith, and History in Orvieto, Italy, and at Laity Lodge in the Texas Hill Country benefited me as I was, respectively, writing early poems and making final arrangements for this volume.

"Contra Belly" is a version of Persius's "Prologus."

"Improbable Rescue of the Heart" is dedicated to Moyra Stiles.

"*Adulescentia*" refers to a common title for coming-of-age books devoted to youth and used in Renaissance classrooms, such as the collection of pastoral verses by Baptista Spagnoli, better known as Mantuan. Belphoebe, mentioned in this poem, refers to one of the great heroines in Edmund Spenser's *The Faerie Queene*.

"Elysium" has for its epigraph a passage from Virgil's *Aeneid*, book 6, when Aeneas first encounters the Elysian fields. The translation is by Robert Fitzgerald.

"Sonnet" personalizes and modernizes Dante's sonnet beginning "Guido, i' vorrei che tu e Lapo ed io[.]" See also Dante Gabriel Rossetti's illustrative oil painting titled *The Boat of Love* (or *The Barque of Love*).

"To David Hooker" is a loosely imitative poem, owing debts of image, voice, and structure to Frank O'Hara's "To John Ashbery" and Allen Ginsberg's "A Supermarket in California."

"The Tree Felled, The Tree Raised" is for Scott Cairns, Leslie Leyland Fields, and Paul Willis.

"Spatulamantic" is for Kimberly Johnson, with a mix of Lucanian grandeur and Jacobean edge that only she could appreciate.